Life Is Short...
BUY THE
BOOTS
and Other
Wonderful Wacky
Words of Wisdom

ISBN: 978-1-68088-072-4

Wonderful Wacky Women®

Inspiring•Uplifting•Empowering

is a trademark of Suzy and Al Toronto. Used under license.

M and Blue Mountain Press are registered in U.S. Patent and Trademark Office. Certain trademarks are used under license.

Printed in China.
Second Printing: 2018

♻ This book is printed on recycled paper.

This book is printed on paper that has been specially produced to be acid free (neutral pH) and contains no groundwood or unbleached pulp. It conforms with the requirements of the American National Standards Institute, Inc., so as to ensure that this book will last and be enjoyed by future generations.

Blue Mountain Arts, Inc.
P.O. Box 4549, Boulder, Colorado 80306

Life Is Short...
BUY THE
BOOTS
and Other
Wonderful Wacky
Words of Wisdom

Suzy Toronto

Blue Mountain Press™
Boulder, Colorado

Life Is a Journey, Not a Race

Stay on the path, even if it means getting your boots a little dirty.

More than once
I've found myself knee-deep
in emotionally stressful messes —
thick, sludgy situations
I'd rather not revisit.
At the time, they seemed
unending, overwhelming,
and unresolvable.

Looking back, I now realize that
as the stresses multiplied,
I began blowing unimportant details
way out of proportion. I allowed myself
to lose sight of the big picture —
missing the beautiful vistas along my path —
and I started leaning on my weaknesses
instead of my strengths.
I ceased focusing on the real issues
and, as a result, slowed down my progress
of getting through the muck
that was destined to be part of my journey.
Now, more than ever, I have resolved
to stay on the path and
not take my eyes off the goal, even if
I have to get my boots dirty along the way.
For life is a journey, not a race.
The ultimate plan is to
keep moving forward
and enjoy the view.

WHEN
TAKING THE
ROAD
LESS
TRAVELED,
IT'S BEST TO WEAR
A ROCKIN' HOT
PAIR OF
BOOTS!

Life is a journey. No one is going to argue with that.
Parts of it are exciting beyond words, beautiful beyond
description, and thrilling beyond our wildest imagination.

As exciting, beautiful, and thrilling
as some parts are, others can be tedious,
strenuous, and even hard to endure.
But our happiness and the journey we are on
should not be measured by the load we bear.
We can choose to pull on
a rockin' hot pair of boots,
pick up our load, and take the unbeaten path.
We can choose to not only travel it
but really live it as well. Relying upon
the merits, mercy, and grace
of the strength within us, we can enjoy
not only the length of our journey
but its width and depth as well.
So take that road less traveled...
and don't forget that rockin' hot pair of boots.
It will make all the difference.
I promise.

Dream Big...
If That Doesn't Work,
Dream Bigger

Have you ever conjured up
a whiz-bang dream,
only to see someone else
living it three months later...
usually selling your idea like hotcakes?
Me too.
Well, the next time it happens, jump on it!
But not just with a little hop.
Plunge on top of it
with everything you've got.
Dream big.
If that doesn't work, dream bigger.
Remember, all great things
started in somebody's basement.

Some of the Best Cowboys Are Not Boys

Boys will be boys. We hear it all the time.
They get all the credit when things are tough,
and they are given permission
to play when it's over...
as if doing their job were reason for reward.
But what about us girls?
We can work just as hard,
play tough, negotiate with skill,
and still dance backward... in high heels!

At the end of the day,
we're not always given credit where credit is due.
So take notice here and now.
I've got news for you:
some of the best cowboys are not boys...
they're girls,
and we'd like to be acknowledged as such.
Whether we're being rough and tough
or pretty as a picture covered with sparkle and bling,
we're 100 percent cowgirl through and through!

© Suzy Toronto

Be Brave Enough to Be Authentic

I dare you,
right here and right now,
to strip yourself down
to the real you —
as strange as it might seem —
and be authentic.
Be willing to sacrifice who you are
for who you could become.

Imagine the freedom
of going through your day
being unapologetically yourself,
marching to your very own beat,
while letting go of the baggage
you thought was necessary to your life.
Embrace the idea that the only person
you are destined to become
is the person you truly are inside.
Be the architect of your own destiny.

As you embrace your authentic self,
your confidence and self-worth will soar.
You will have the courage to stand a little taller
and reach a little farther than ever before.
And your example will encourage
others to do the same.
Go ahead. Give it a try!
I dare you.

©Suzy Toronto

Don't Let Anyone Dull Your Sparkle

© Suzy Toronto

Is it genetics or just a fluke of nature?
Regardless, some of us are simply
born with glitter in our veins.
Whether we're sparkling like the noonday sun
or bubbling with so much enthusiasm that
we leave a virtual bubble bath in our wake,
the whole spectacle is out of our control.
However, it's a condition that those of us
who are affected have come to embrace.

So please, don't let anyone
try to dull your sparkle…
or tell you to "tone it down"…
or ask you to restrain yourself.
If they do, your only recourse is to
grab a can of spray adhesive with one hand
and a jar of glitter with the other
and proceed to cover them
with a lavish coat of sticky, iridescent bling.
So let your life sparkle and shine,
and embrace all the glitter within you.

yes ...as a matter of fact, I DO need another pair of **boots!**

There are a few things in life where the line between need and want is hard to define.

Fortunately, when it comes to boots,
there is no problem.
The answer is always crystal clear.
That's because you can
NEVER have too many
amazingly awesome,
incredibly adorable,
rockin' hot boots.
Quite simply, a new pair of kickers
envelops me with a sense of confidence
with just the right amount of sass and class.
They give me my superpower
and make me feel invincible.
(Not to mention they totally
make my heart tingle!)

So yes, as a matter of fact,
I *do* need another pair of boots!

Release Your Inner Child

As children, we were invincible.
We could do anything we dreamed up!
The world was our canvas, and there was
no end to the possibilities we could kick up.

As we grew older, that youthful spirit faded.
We worried way too much about
what other people thought, and we began
to question our own talents and abilities.

But now, if you look deep inside your heart
(buried under years of growing pains!),
you can still find that unbridled, childlike conviction.
It's there — and it's real.
It fans the flames of dreams,
creativity, and imagination.

So release your inner child
and believe in yourself again.
There's more inside you
than you ever dreamed possible!

© Suzy Toronto

Boots
and
Bling...

They're a
Cowgirl
Thing!

I was born with a soul
that is country through and through.
I love the smell of fresh country air,
the sway of a front porch swing
and the refreshing taste of ice-cold sweet tea.
And when it comes to the things
I surround myself with,
I include the sounds of rockin' country vibes,
adorable boots that make my heart tingle,
and a bit of bling to make it all sparkle.

Like lightning bugs on a hot summer's eve,
I love daisy bouquets and
pretty, girly things
that glitter and shine.
From the top of my cowgirl hat
to the tips of my pointy-toed boots,
I want to shimmer.

Bottom line is this:
boots and bling...
they're just a cowgirl thing.

How to Use the
Pointy End
of Your
Boot

Life is all about
give and take.
But some issues
simply cannot
be compromised.
When the situation
calls for drastic measures,
you have to be willing
to use the pointy end
of your kicker
to protect the hill
you're willing
to die on.

It's not going to be easy...
anything worth fighting for never is.
But the most noble thing you can do
is stand up for what is right, no matter the cost.
So dust off your boots and use these
step-by-step instructions
as you head into battle...

1. Stomp one foot loudly so that
   everyone knows you mean business.
2. Throw a "hissie fit" with exact timing
   and precision, leaving no doubt as to
   where you stand.
3. In a hushed whisper, point to the toe
   of your boot and inform folks you intend
   to use the pointy end if this nonsense
   is not resolved immediately.

That's it. That's all there is to it!
You never have to actually describe what
you're going to do with the toe of your kicker.
I promise you, it works every time.
So never, ever underestimate the
power of a pointy pair of boots.

© Suzy Toronto

When You
Stumble,
Make It Part
of the
Dance

Everyone messes up.
It's part of the dance of life.
But when those obstacles
become tough to negotiate,
it's inevitable that
we'll stumble.

Despite the fact that the music plays on,
we find ourselves out of step and
desperately searching for a "do over" button.
That's when creativity and adaptability become
our most valuable, lifesaving virtues.
They help us to act as if it were all
part of the show... even though
we may feel our pride is a bit bruised.
Without offering apologies or excuses,
the trick is to just
continue onward,
with all our heart and soul,
as if our lives depended on it.

So the next time you stumble,
smile at the crowd,
kick up your heels,
and dance a do-si-do.
The moment you embrace it
as your own, no one will know
it's not part of *your* dance.

© Suzy Toronto

BOOTS
make your
TOES
feel like
THEY'RE IN THE
COUNTRY

Some of us are
lucky enough to live
the country life while
others only get to visit.
Regardless, there are times
when we all must pretend
to tolerate the city
even though
our hearts know better.

It is essential to own a pair of the
cutest, most irresistibly adorable pair of boots
to get us through just such a predicament.
All we need to do is slip them on and click our heels.
In the blink of an eye, we would then be transported
to a majestic mountain retreat...
a prairie with amber waves of grain...
or a red rock desert mesa.
The trials of being away from our
beloved country life
would be instantly soothed.
Our hearts would be blissfully
lifted away by the sensation of our toes
being caressed by the soft, supple leather
of a rockin' hot pair of wacky western boots.

With a power like that,
wacky western boots could easily
become the new dress standard.
Bottom line: boots really do
make your toes feel like
they're in the country.

Wonderful Wacky Words
to Make Your Heart Tingle

Life is too short to wear pantyhose ◎ If you want rainbows, you gotta have rain ◎ Don't play life safe; make waves ◎ Enthusiasm is contagious ◎ Life is all about how you handle Plan B... in the end, it's the true test of character ◎ Art does not have to match your sofa, your hair color... or your boots ◎

Play with wild abandon 🌀 Happiness is always
an inside job 🌀 When life gets crazy, do
something normal... and if life gets too
normal, do something crazy 🌀 No one's
last words were ever "I wish I'd eaten more
celery sticks" 🌀 When life gets stormy, pull
on your boots and go out looking for puddles
to play in 🌀 Dream with your eyes wide open 🌀
And the most important thing to know...
age is nothing but a state of mind 🌀
So pick an age you like,
and stick to it! 🌀

© Suzy Toronto

Kick Off Your Boots...

Feel the Tingle of Just Being Home

There are few places on earth that can rival
home. Sure, there are places to visit
with rugged majestic mountains
or tropical pounding surf that have
the power to positively take our breath away.
Yet when the visit is over, the bottom line
is that there is simply no place like home.

© Suzy Toronto

Home is that one place on earth where you
know you belong, where comfort is a given
and your very heart seems to beat in sync
to the energy of its surroundings.

But really, is home a place or a state of mind?
Perhaps if we search within ourselves deep enough,
we'll see that home is not, in fact, a physical location
but rather a feeling, an attitude, and a sense of belonging
that is deep within our heart and soul.
Tapping into this state of mind allows us
to feel the sense of love and the security of home,
no matter where our journey takes us.
The next time you're homesick and
longing for familiar surroundings,
take a deep breath, close your eyes,
and transport your mind back to that place
that can only be described as pure comfort.
Visualize it. Feel it. Smell it.
And most of all, enjoy it.
Once you master this trick,
you'll never be homesick again.

21 Wacky Ways to Develop Your God-Given Gifts

1. Reach outside your comfort zone
2. Color outside the lines
3. Carry yourself with confidence
4. Seek wisdom
5. Don't be afraid to be a triple mocha in a world full of vanilla
6. Be responsible for the mojo you bring into the room
7. Expand your horizons
8. Read good books
9. Speak with conviction
10. Let your imagination soar

11. Believe that your future does not lie ahead of you; it lies deep inside you
12. Don't let someone who gave up on their dreams talk you out of yours
13. Choose the right thing... even when it's not the easiest choice
14. Develop an attitude of gratitude
15. Live with integrity
16. Make your life and your actions a story worth telling
17. Stay focused... you only see obstacles when you take your eyes off the goal
18. Choose to make virtue a habit
19. Dream in colors that do not yet exist
20. Create the life you've always wanted
21. Always believe that something fabulously amazing is going to happen

© Suzy Toronto

Kindness Never Goes out of Style

Life is never going to be perfect.
Conflicts are bound to arise
and challenges will inevitably come.
A lot of it is simply out of our control.
But the only things we *can* control
are our attitude and
how we deal with it.

We can choose to be whiny,
hardheaded, and selfish,
or we can choose to be kind,
considerate, and understanding.

Whenever you can, choose the latter.
When challenges arise,
choose to take a deep breath,
try to see the other point of view,
and resolve things with civility.
Strive to be kind…
especially when it isn't easy,
because you will never regret
being too kind.

©Suzy Toronto

No one wants to be constantly saying
"would've, should've, could've"...
forever looking back, second-guessing every decision,
and fretting over what might have been.
Yet it's funny how we can cling to the past,
thinking that we can maybe find a "do over" button
and create a whole different ending.
All this does is fill us with guilt and regret
and turn our resolve to live a life worth truly loving
into a quivering mass of jello. Yuck!

Well, I have a news flash for you.
The past is over!
Nothing you do will ever change that.
So let go and break free!
Start this very moment by honoring
your individual worth and accepting
responsibility for your choices.
Release the old, embrace the new,
and make today — right here and
right now — your focus.
Now is the time for you to live your life
like you really mean it
and finally evolve into the magnificent free spirit
you always intended to be.

© Suzy Toronto

Life Is Short...
BUY THE
BOOTS

Life is filled with uncertainty.
Good times come and go.
But when the low points hit us,
sometimes it's hard to
put a smile on our faces and move on.
That's why I buy cute boots!

When I'm having a bad day,
I can always run to my closet,
slip on a pair of wildly hot, totally rockin',
knock-your-socks-off boots, and suddenly
everything around me gets brighter.
Not only does it make me smile,
but everyone who sees me smiles too.

Okay, so I have a few pairs of boots...
all right, maybe more than a few,
but they just make me so happy.
Besides, they are not immoral,
illegal, or fattening,
and they make my heart tingle.

So follow my lead. Go ahead...
buy the boots.
After all, life is short.

©Suzy Toronto

About the Author

So this is me... I'm a tad wacky and just shy of crazy. I'm fiftysomething and live in the sleepy village of Tangerine, Florida, with my husband, Al, and a big, goofy dog named Lucy. And because life wasn't crazy enough, my eightysomething-year-old parents live with us too. (In my home, the nuts don't fall far from the tree!) I eat far too much chocolate, and I drink sparkling water by the gallon. I practice yoga, ride a little red scooter, and go to the beach every chance I get. I have five grown children and over a dozen grandkids who love me as much as I adore them. I teach them to dip their French fries in their chocolate shakes and to make up any old words to the tunes they like. But most of all, I teach them to never, ever color inside the lines. This is the Wild Wacky Wonderful life I lead, and I wouldn't have it any other way. Welcome to my world!